I0118153

THE BIOLOGY OF GOVERNMENT

A PRIMER FOR POLITICIANS

GREG LAWRENCE

VIVID

PUBLISHING

Copyright © 2013 Gregory James Lawrence

Published by Vivid Publishing
A division of the Fontaine Publishing Group
P.O. Box 948 Fremantle
Western Australia 6959
www.vividpublishing.com.au

National Library of Australia Cataloguing-in-Publication data:
Author: Lawrence, Greg, author.
Title: The biology of government / Greg Lawrence.
ISBN: 9781922204677 (paperback)
Subjects: Environmental management--Social aspects.
            Sustainable development--Environmental aspects.
            Environmental policy.
            Environmental protection.
            Government accountability.
Dewey Number: 333.7

All rights reserved. This publication may be reproduced only in limited form
for educational or review purposes, as allowable by Australian copyright law.
Please contact the author for permission to reporoduce in expanded form.

This book is also available as an eBook edition.
For further information about this book please visit:
www.vividpublishing.com.au/thebiologyofgovernment

To my parents, Jim and Pat, who provided the right mix of support and freedom to their three sons.

CONTENTS

"The creation of appearances is now far more important for leading politicians than is the generation of outcomes. This produces a good deal of deception, and an approach that I call 'the politics of the moment'. Winning today's micro-argument is all important, and tomorrow can look after itself."

—Lindsay Tanner, former Australian Minister for Finance and Deregulation.

1
THE ROLE

Question: What is the role of government?

Answer: To look to the well-being of the people and to maintain and improve the quality of the environment.

Government is animal husbandry and ecosystem management.

Government is applied biology.

2
THE DREAM

Let's dream.

A country.

A government composed of individuals who see their job as managing a complex society in a complex environment for the well-being of the people and their descendants.

A government composed of individuals who are not prepared to compromise good management for short-term electoral gain and/or to selectively benefit themselves, their supporters, friends or family – that is, a government that is not corrupt.

A government composed of individuals who make decisions based on a rational, evidence-based and, when appropriate, scientific assessment of each situation that comes before it – that is, it does not allow ideology to prescribe its decisions.

3

The Dream Continued

Let us continue the dream.

A country.

An ethical government with a mission statement:

"Look to the well-being of the people."

But how?

Looking to the well-being of the people means providing an environment that satisfies the needs of the people.

Therefore, the first step to good government is knowing the needs of the people.

The second step is creating and maintaining an environment that provides these needs.

4

STEP 1

If the first step of good government is knowing the needs of the people, we need to ask what these needs are.

They will be considered in two categories: those required for the well-being of the body and those required for the well-being of the mind.

Strictly, such a division should not be made, since the well-being of the body is not independent of the well-being of the mind, and vice versa. For instance, the mind can influence the biochemistry of the body.

Nevertheless, considering the tangible needs of the physical body separately from the less tangible needs of the mind has value.

It should be noted that not every individual has exactly the same needs, since some needs can vary depending on age, sex and genetic make-up (which is sometimes associated with ethnic origin).

5
THE BODY

The body needs an environment that provides:

- Food.
- Water.
- Protection from the elements (clothing, shelter, heat source).
- An atmosphere with an oxygen content of approximately 21 per cent, in which the carbon dioxide level is between 280 and 330 parts per million (for optimum climate) and that is largely free of toxic gases and injurious airborne pollutants.
- An atmosphere that has a pressure at sea level of approximately one kilogram per square centimetre (14.7 pounds per square inch).
- A stratosphere with sufficient ozone to absorb most of the incoming ultraviolet light.
- A suitable temperature.
- A suitable gravity pull.
- Light (to develop and maintain eye function).

For children, strong light (outdoors) for two to three hours a day to prevent myopia.

- Distant views (may be necessary for the development of all-round vision in children).

- A day–night sequence based on a 24-hour cycle (to maintain biorhythms).

- Sunlight with ultraviolet light (for vitamin D production by skin cells to promote calcium uptake, thereby preventing rickets in children and weak bones in older people, and to reduce the chances of developing multiple sclerosis, diabetes and some types of cancer that can occur if insufficient vitamin D is present in the diet).

- A certain amount of "dirt" (necessary for a strong and properly developed immune system) and, for children, to make them more resistant to allergies.

- Opportunities for exercise.

- Conditions that do not promote disease (e.g. living conditions should not be unsanitary and crowded, drinking water should be free of faecal contamination and efforts should be made to reduce the numbers of insects that transmit disease).

- No exposure, or only low-level exposure, to drugs and injurious chemicals (man made or natural), heavy metals, radioactive materials, asbestos fibres and high levels of noise for extended periods.

- Access to quality medical care that all can afford.
- Conditions that satisfy the needs of the mind (see next chapter).

6

THE MIND

What are the requirements of the mind?

The needs of the mind are more difficult to define than those of the body. However, it would appear that the following things are important for most people:

- Interaction and communication with other people.

- Belonging to a true community, which can provide companionship, support and security, particularly for older people.

- Someone to love and care for.
  Someone to be loved by, and cared for by.
  Someone to have sex and orgasms with.[1]

- Having children, which can give joy, purpose and meaning to life.

- Having time to spend with one's children.

- Being valued and considered an individual of

---

1 Studies have found that women vary greatly in their ability to achieve orgasms, with approximately one in six never achieving an orgasm. Some women only achieve orgasms after childbirth or when they reach their late twenties. Twin studies have shown that a significant amount of this variation is due to genetic differences.

worth by one's fellow human beings.

- Having a job, feeling useful.

- Having time to help others and/or to support community causes, which typically generates a strong sense of well-being and happiness in the giver.

- An environment in which fun and laughter are frequent occurrences.

- Physical exercise.

- Mental activities.

- A diverse sensory environment, providing abundant opportunities for sight, sound, touch, smell and taste experiences.

- Adequate time for sleeping, preferably during the night.

- Some association with the natural world (even if just gardening or keeping a pet animal).

- If life is mostly hectic, time to slow down and relax and to participate in play and leisure activities.

- The freedom to choose to belong to a religion or not to belong to a religion.

- An environment that provides universal education and diverse job opportunities, so that most people can find a job suited to their nature and abilities and which gives satisfaction.

- An equal society, so that a sense of injustice is not engendered in some individuals.

- Occasional periods of stress, pressure and hardship, which may be beneficial, even necessary, by providing diversity to the experience of life and by imparting wisdom, maturity and a self-confidence to manage the hard times (physical and mental) in life should they arise unexpectedly.

- For children, love and affection from parents and other adults who set reasonable standards in a secure environment, and opportunities for play and for physical and mental activities (all important for a child's physical, intellectual and emotional development).

- Conditions that provide all the needs of the body.

7
KIDS

Kids are important. Kids are the product of their genes and the environment. Kids have no control over either of these elements. Therefore, those that do – parents, politicians and public policymakers – have a special responsibility for their care and provision. Influences early in life can determine physical and mental characteristics – both positive and negative – that last throughout life.

Genes

When a sperm carrying one set of genes fuses with an egg carrying another set of genes, an embryo is created with a unique combination of genes. As revealed by comparisons of genetically identical twins with genetically non-identical twins, genes play a major role in determining the physical characteristics, nature and interests of the human being that arises from an embryo. Under natural circumstances, the fusion of a particular sperm with a particular egg is a chance event and cannot be influenced.

However, something can be done about the quality of the DNA in the egg and the sperm. How? By having children while young and avoiding agents that damage DNA. Women are born with a lifetime supply of eggs, but it appears that the quality of the eggs may decline with age based on the observation that the firstborn child of a young woman has a greater chance of living to age 100 than later children do. In addition, the eggs of older women are more likely to contain chromosomal abnormalities, which in the case of an additional copy of chromosome 21 gives rise to Down syndrome. Eggs have enzymes to repair any damage to their DNA that may occur while they are in storage, but the amount of these enzymes declines with age. This may be why the eggs of young women appear to be of higher quality than those of older women.

Men constantly produce new sperm cells, but the germ cells that give rise to sperm accumulate mutations as men age. A study carried out in Iceland found that a 20-year-old father transmits, on average, 25 new mutations to his child, whereas a 40-year-old father transmits around 65. Children of older men (those over 45 to 50) are more likely to suffer congenital defects involving the heart, spine and limbs as well as being more likely to suffer from Down syndrome, autism, schizophrenia and epilepsy. Thus, there are good reasons for both sexes to have children early in their reproductive life rather than later.

To avoid possible DNA damage to sperm, men should limit caffeine consumption because increased genetic damage has been found in the sperm of men who consume average amounts of caffeine (three cups a day). Smoking should also be avoided since it can directly damage DNA, as well as reduce sperm quantity and vigour, and cause impotence. Sperm quality can also be reduced by a diet high in fat, a diet lacking in antioxidants (fruit and vegetables), and excessive exercise, alcohol, drugs, stress and environmental pollution.

Obese men should lose weight, since recent studies with rodents have shown that paternal obesity, or the high-calorie diet that caused the obesity, increases the susceptibility to obesity and diabetes in offspring. If this effect also occurs in humans, an individual fathered by an obese man may have a greater chance of being overweight and affected by diabetes than an individual fathered by the same man if of normal weight. In one mouse study it was found that the expression level of 445 genes appeared to depend strongly on the diet of the father. In addition to carrying a set of genes made from DNA (deoxyribonucleic acid), mouse sperm contain small molecules of RNA (ribonucleic acid), which can vary with changes in the weight of the male mouse producing the sperm. Since these small RNA molecules (which are also found in human sperm) are involved in regulating the level at which genes are expressed, differences in these molecules could be responsible for the finding that the offspring of an obese male mouse have a greater chance of suffering negative health effects than those fathered by a mouse of normal weight.

Environment

Three periods need to be considered when examining the effect of environmental factors on a child's development: (1) the period before conception and the first three weeks of pregnancy, (2) the period of pregnancy and (3) the period after birth. Prospective parents can receive sound advice for all of these stages from general practitioners, various specialists and the many websites and books that have been written on the topic. Therefore, only the principal biological factors that are relevant to all prospective parents are considered below.

1. The period before conception and the first three weeks of pregnancy:

The first three weeks of pregnancy are included here because a woman will not usually know that she is pregnant until three to four weeks after conception. Therefore, couples seeking a pregnancy need to behave as though a pregnancy has been achieved.

For the mother-to-be, a visit to a doctor for a general health check, including blood pressure, glucose levels and rubella immunity, is recommended. Advice should be sought in taking medication and drugs since many, including caffeine and alcohol, can pass through the placenta.

Prior to conception, if either of the parents-to-be is overweight, there are benefits to be had from restoring weight to normal levels. For the prospective father, these relate to the influence that weight may have on the type of small RNA molecules present in the sperm, as outlined above. As well, there is evidence that obesity is associated with reduced sperm quality. Male fertility can be maximised by not smoking, eating well (including plenty of fruit and vegetables), having an adequate daily intake of zinc (good sources being seafood, green-leafy vegetables, cereals and beans), drinking alcohol in moderation (or not at all) and getting plenty of (moderate) exercise. For the prospective mother, being overweight increases the likelihood of complications during pregnancy, including developing gestational diabetes, which can have serious lifelong effects on the developing child. Being overweight can also stop ovulation.

For the mother-to-be, a folic acid supplement, beginning one month prior to conception, is usually recommended to reduce the risk of neural tube defects. An iodine supplement may also be recommended if natural intake is below the recommended level, as it often is. If necessary, now is the time to develop healthy eating habits, since good nutrition is required during pregnancy. Heavy drinking of alcohol should be avoided. Smoking reduces the chances of a woman becoming pregnant. Moderate exercise is nearly always beneficial.

2. *The period of pregnancy:*

Good nutrition should be maintained throughout pregnancy to reduce the chances of an underweight baby. Severe under-nutrition during pregnancy can affect the activity settings of some genes (such as boosting the activity of fat-storing genes) in the developing foetus that can last a lifetime. During early pregnancy, folic acid (and iodine) supplementation should be continued. Any iodine supplement should not be derived from kelp because this may contain mercury. Throughout pregnancy, a diet high in iron, calcium, iodine and folate is recommended. Vitamins B12 and D, iron, calcium and folic acid (beyond the first three months) supplements may be recommended to a pregnant woman who is a vegan or vegetarian, who is carrying two or more foetuses or who lives in a low-light environment. However, vitamins should not be taken in excess; this especially applies to vitamin A, an oversupply of which can harm the foetus. Drinking milk, which provides calcium and vitamin D, during pregnancy appears to be beneficial, providing protective effects to the mother and slightly increased birth weight to the baby. In one study, children of mothers who had low vitamin D levels in their blood during their second and third trimesters were twice as likely to have speech-learning difficulties.

Pregnant women should avoid foods that may contain the bacterium *Listeria monocytogenes*, such as soft cheeses, pâtés, non-pasteurised milk, soft-serve ice cream, cold deli-style meats and pre-prepared salads, since infection with this bacterium can cause a miscarriage or an infection in the newborn baby. Pregnant women should also avoid alcohol completely; not smoke, because smoking increases the risk of miscarriage, stillbirth, malformation and low birth weight of the baby; take insulin if diabetic; and, if asthmatic, try to avoid acute asthma attacks because this can have a detrimental effect on the baby. In the third trimester, women should avoid sleeping on their backs because this slightly increases the chance of a stillbirth.

Vaccination against influenza is recommended by

health care authorities because there is an increased risk of flu complications, including pneumonia, during pregnancy and because it provides immunity to the baby for the first six months of life. Vaccination against whooping cough should be considered (if the mother is not already vaccinated) since young babies whose mothers have been vaccinated are 50 per cent less likely than other infants to contract the illness (which can be fatal to young babies).

High stress levels in the mother-to-be should also be avoided because this can have negative effects on the baby's development leading to later problems such as attention deficit hyperactivity disorder. Women showing symptoms of stress are three times more likely to miscarry in the first three weeks of gestation. Moderate exercise is likely to be beneficial.

3. The period after birth:

The World Health Organization currently recommends breastfeeding for the first six months after birth followed by a mix of solids and breastfeeding for the following six months. The first solids should include iron-rich foods because the iron stores built up during pregnancy are starting to deplete after six months. Some breastfeeding can be continued for up to two, three, four and even five years, providing benefits to both the mother and the baby. Breastfed

babies have lower rates of ear infections, eczema, di-
arrhoea, sudden infant death syndrome, obesity, leu-
kaemia and childhood diabetes. Breast milk contains
immune factors that protect babies against infection
while their own immune systems are still developing
– a protection that apparently continues after a baby
is weaned. Breast milk also contains long-chain poly-
unsaturated fatty acids that build brain tissue. Babies
breastfed for more than six months subsequently
have lower rates of delinquent, aggressive and antisocial behaviour and, overall, are less depressed, anx-
ious and withdrawn. Mothers who breastfeed have
lower rates of breast cancer and ovarian cancer, and
the longer they breastfeed, the lower the rates.

At night, babies should be placed on their backs
to sleep. However, during the day babies should be
placed, on some occasions, on their fronts during
times of play. This helps to develop the neck and arm
muscles and to prevent head deformation. Babies
should be placed on their tummies for the first time
within five days of birth. If left later than this, the
baby may consider the tummy position abnormal and
become upset.

Babies and young children should be given all
the recommended vaccinations at the recommended
times.

Circumcision of boys? This is a matter of parental

choice; however, circumcised males are protected against foreskin constriction and have fewer penile inflammatory conditions, fewer urinary tract and kidney infections, less prostate cancer and are less likely to catch the AIDS virus or syphilis. In addition, their female partners are less likely to develop cervical cancer. Circumcision does not reduce sexual enjoyment.

Once a child is walking, leaving him or her barefoot as much as possible is good for foot development.

Children raised in excessively clean environments are more likely to develop allergies than those raised in dirtier environments. Outdoor play is good. Children raised in the company of a dog for the first two years of life are less likely to develop an allergy. Limited exposure of the skin to sunlight is beneficial for vitamin D production, but exposure to amounts sufficient to burn the skin should be avoided. One-year-old infants deficient in vitamin D are more likely to have one or more food allergies than infants with normal vitamin D levels. Children should not be exposed to cigarette smoke.

Children should spend two to three hours outdoors each day to prevent myopia (nearsightedness). The bright light outdoors stimulates dopamine release, which stops the eyeball from growing elongated and distorting the focus of light entering the eye. Physical activity is also good for the eyes because it stimulates wider arterioles (and therefore, better blood supply) in the retina. Having distant views may help develop all-round vision.

Parental care or group care? Studies show that parental care for the first two or three years is best, although subsequent academic performance appears not to be harmed by early group care (based on a British study). From three years on, children are social animals and can thrive in group care. Parents should not be overly attentive. At age three, a child should be looking to the parent, not expecting the parent to be looking to him or her. The latter situation can lead to negative outcomes. Overprotective parents may slow brain growth of children and increase the risk of mental illness. Parents should not argue or fight in front of their children – even babies of a few months – because this can distress them greatly.

From birth onwards, picture books and bedtime stories, spending plenty of time outdoors in nature and socialising with a mix of other adults and children are all beneficial. As noted in *New Scientist* (4 April 2009), "a nurturing environment, one-on-one playtime with games like peekaboo, building blocks, singing nursery rhymes and shape-sorting are all a child needs to increase IQ and foster a lifelong interest in learning" and "the most important factor in language development is how much a parent talks to the child after birth, the complexity of their vocabulary and how well they focus the child's attention".

8

Raising Kids - In Brief

Like them.

Spend time with them.

Do not treat them as useless nothings.

Treat them as beings of worth

(but do not treat them like little emperors).

Have a few reasonable standards.

Let them know what those standards are.

Set an example by keeping to those standards yourself – and hope that fate does not deal out too many unkind cards.

There are no guarantees.

Promoting intelligence

In response to a question on how to make kids as intelligent as possible, Jane Barry, a child health nurse, provided the following answer (*Canberra Times*, 6 April 2010):

Babies are born with around 10 billion neurons in their brains, just poised to absorb as much stimulation as possible. Their brains are pliable and literally moulded by the interactions and experiences to which they are exposed. This, combined with their individual potential and the genes they inherit from parents, all influence intelligence. It pays to remember that the system is designed to succeed, despite parents' concern and angst. Kids are excellent at sourcing stimulating experiences, and given a secure enough environment, they generally do very well. It's valuable for parents to provide a rich and varied home life, rather than one which is insulated or exclusive. Children thrive in homes where music, conversation, language and colour are part of everyday life. Parents who show affection to each other as well as their children teach the value of emotional intimacy, a quality so important it can't be overstated. Foster in them a love of learning and inquisitiveness. Curious children tend to be bright and good problem solvers. They also attract attention, which will help their intellect. Play is intrinsically linked to learning, so *make sure they have plenty of opportunity for games and fun. Physical activity needs to be encouraged, but aim for a balance with quiet play times as well. Read to them, with them and for them. Children always benefit from books and literacy. Work at maintaining your own brain function and intellect. Try not to invest everything you have into parenting them – you need to retain some interests just for yourself. From this they can only benefit.*

9
SNAPSHOTS

Climbing 1

Eleven kids, two adults on a seven-kilometre walk in the Australian bush. After two or three kilometres, the youngest child, a girl about three and a half years old, gets tired. Asked if she would like a ride on the shoulders of one of the adults, she says yes. One or two kilometres later, the group comes to a creek that is easy to cross because it contains just a trickle of water. The incline on the other side of the creek, the beginning of a cliff line, is steep – too steep to walk up without using the hands. However, there are numerous rock outcrops and many tree saplings, providing ample holds, so climbing is not that difficult. The older kids tackle the climb with enthusiasm. The young girl on the shoulders of the adult says nothing, but starts to wriggle vigorously, making it very clear that she wants to be put back on the ground. Once on the ground, she runs to the incline and starts climbing.

Kids like a physical challenge. They should not be forced to take them, but they should not be denied the opportunity. Climbing seems to have special appeal.

Climbing 2

Mother and nine-year-old daughter set out to climb an 800-metre mountain following a track to the top. Daughter is not happy: "This is boring". The track unexpectedly ends – by mistake, the pair had followed a new track still under construction. The decision is made to continue straight up the mountain off the track. This involves rock scrambling in some places and negotiating some very steep sections through bushes and trees. Daughter loves the challenge. Daughter is no longer bored. Daughter is happy.

Climbing 3

Twelve kids on a camp go fishing from a pier. Some fish halfway along the pier – the remainder near the end of the pier. While two accompanying adults are with the first group, a 10-year-old girl in the second group snags a hook on her line on one of the piles down at the water's edge. Girl decides to free her line. She climbs over the side onto a crossbeam. Halfway down this crossbeam, she switches to the crossbeam coming from the top of the opposite pile on the other side of the pier, which takes her down to where the hook is snagged. Once the hook is freed, the girl returns via the same route. However, on reaching the top of the crossbeam, the girl finds it difficult to get around the edge of the pier and pull herself onto its upper surface, so the two adults, who had returned to this group by now, take a hand each and haul the girl vertically upwards onto the pier. Girl is completely unperturbed – episode over, fishing continues. This girl, balanced and sensible – certainly not reckless or stupid – enjoyed a challenge.

10
PRACTICE

Theory is neat; practice is messy.

So what to do? The aim of any government should be clear: create an environment that provides all the factors necessary for the well-being of all its citizens. These factors are known and they are outlined above.

In practice, resources are always limited, so priorities should be determined by the current state of affairs. If a significant proportion of the population in a country is malnourished, lacks adequate shelter and is suffering from disease, obviously, these areas should have first call on the resources of the government.

Governments should educate. Education for all – girls as well as boys – is essential in both developed and developing countries. It opens up so many opportunities for the individual and economic benefits for the government. Teachers should be valued: they have one of the most important jobs in any society. It has been found that a good teacher trumps socio-economic status, class size, curriculum design and parents' educational levels in determining academic achievement. Governments should recognise this. It is a tragedy when a good teacher gives up teaching because of low pay, poor conditions, lack of recognition or the need to do large amounts of unpaid overtime.

Governments should inform. No student should leave school without a full knowledge of human biology and how environmental factors influence that biology and affect health and well-being. All school leavers should know the requirements of a balanced diet and be aware of the consequences of an excessive intake of energy-rich foods, lack of exercise, smoking, drinking alcohol in excess and taking drugs. They should know about sexually transmitted diseases and how they are contracted. Factors important for a healthy pregnancy should be known to all. A woman who drinks alcohol during pregnancy should at least know that she may be harming her foetus. Perhaps every student leaving school should be given a handbook on human biology, lifestyle and health.

Along with education, health should be a major area of concern to all governments. Since "prevention is better than cure", governments should give adequate attention and funding to preventing health problems – many fail in this respect. In developing countries, areas that should be high on a government's list of priorities include preventing malnourishment; providing safe drinking and washing water; providing improved medical services before, during and after childbirth; vaccination programs; reducing the consumption of tobacco and other drugs; improving the safety of work places; reducing deaths and injury from road accidents; and improving air quality in the home by promoting alternatives to wood fires and kerosene stoves and lamps.

In developed countries, many of the issues just listed may not be a problem, but governments need to ensure that the funding and services that make these issues "not a problem" are maintained. Tobacco and drug use and excessive alcohol consumption impose huge costs on many societies and should be a priority target of all governments. An emerging problem in developed societies is the excessive consumption of energy-rich foods and sugar-rich drinks, which, when combined with a lack of exercise, has led to a large proportion of some populations being overweight and unfit. This is a major health problem – increased rates of diabetes, heart attacks and strokes will follow, leading to a large increase in health costs. It surely is time for governments to wage a war on obesity. But, so far, weak-willed governments have done little more than to initiate a skirmish or two.

As a first step, governments should ban, or

severely curtail, the advertising of harm-causing products such as tobacco, alcohol and energy-rich foods and drink. Price increases should be considered since it is well established that increasing the price of these products reduces consumption. For example, a tax on soft drinks introduced in Hungary in 2011 reduced sales by 41 per cent.

Governments should not just encourage exercise but promote it in every way possible – given that it is so important for both physical and mental health. For kids, exercise helps to develop a healthy heart, lungs, bones and eyes, and is one of the few measures known to delay early puberty in girls. For adults, exercise reduces the likelihood of heart attack, stroke, diabetes and being overweight. Mentally, it reduces stress and, based on some recent evidence, reduces the likelihood of dementia as a person ages. Overweight people who are fit are much less likely to suffer adverse health effects than those who are not. Exercise triggers the release of chemicals in the brain that elevate mood and reduce pain and anxiety. People can become addicted. Governments should encourage their citizens to become addicted, or at least to experience the general sense of well-being that comes from being fit. Lazing about doing nothing is much more enjoyable when one is fit than when one is unfit. An unfit populace is costly in both economic and social terms, and the cost increases as people age. Governments really cannot afford not to promote fitness in their citizens.

So, how to cultivate fitness without compulsory boot camps? School curricula should contain periods for sport or physical activity. School playgrounds should entice students into physical activity during lunch and recess times. Every community should have easy access to sports fields and playgrounds. Politicians who sell off playing fields and open space to developers for a one-off monetary windfall, or who allow new housing developments to proceed without adequate provision of sports grounds and play areas, should be condemned and voted out of office. They will have diminished the lives of many generations of citizens. There should be bicycle paths wherever possible, preferably separated from road traffic; they should be included in every new greenfield housing development. People who use public transport usually walk more each day than those that use a car – another reason for having an efficient public transport system that will encourage greater use.

In developed countries, many children are exercising less outside school hours due to the increasing amount of time spent playing computer games, watching television and networking on social media. This is likely to reduce fitness levels and increase health risks – risks that will be greatly increased if a child is also overweight.

So, how to lure kids away from their screens? One possibility – old-style adventure playgrounds of the type popular in Britain in the decades after World War II, where kids can build playhouses, dig holes, light fires, cook food, swing from ropes or do any other unstructured activity that takes their fancy. A roofed area with some tables and chairs, a fence to hide the mess, a water supply and an adult or two for supervision (only if required) are the minimal requirements. Such places were once very popular with kids. They could be again. Based on the British experience, adventure playgrounds of this type are remarkably safe places, involving minimal accidents.

Possibility two: excursion groups. Many years ago, the social action group at a university initiated several community-orientated activities in a nearby neighbourhood. One of these was "Sunday club" – kids of various ages and both sexes would meet on Sunday afternoon at a local park and then be taken, by minibus and car, to sites, usually within 50 kilometres, suited to unstructured, nature-based activities. Thus, in hot weather, the excursion would usually be to a beach for a swim. At other times, short walks in the hills, visiting waterfalls and dams, exploring creeks and looking for frogs, mudslides down creek banks,

bicycle riding along dirt fire-access roads and light-
ing a fire in a disused quarry to toast marshmallows
were some of the activities undertaken. It is clear the
kids enjoyed these activities since they kept turning
up, and their parents (often a single parent) no doubt
appreciated a child-free afternoon. Once a year, this
group would also go on a four-day camp at a more
distant location. Unstructured activities such as these
are enjoyed by kids and benefit them in subtle ways.

Older kids and teenagers become more selective
in their activities. Therefore, as much choice as possible should be available so they can find something
that appeals to them. Most sports require some infrastructure to play, and governments should provide as
much of this as possible. This requires a significant
commitment by governments, given the large variety of sports that might be catered for, such as the
various football codes, baseball, basketball, netball,
cricket, hockey, lacrosse, the various racquet games,
volleyball, bowling and bowls, athletics, swimming,
cycling, surfing, diving, gymnastics, martial arts, ice
and roller-skating, skiing, snowboarding, kayaking,
rowing, sailing, archery, shooting, horse riding, danc-
ing, rock climbing and hiking. Ideally, each neighbourhood should have a high-quality skateboard
park where anyone can drop in for no charge for
any length of time. Older kids and young teenagers

do not have drivers' licences, so good bicycle paths, particularly leading to schools, will promote exercise and independence, reduce vehicle use and, in some cases, free up parents' time. Since, in many societies, teenage girls often stop playing sport, particular efforts should be made to keep them doing some form of physical activity.

Governments should work with biology, not against it. Couples often delay having children because of a perceived need to establish a career or build up a deposit for a house before doing so. Governments should work to remove these factors because there are clear benefits to both mother and child for couples to have children while they are younger. If excessive amounts of homework severely limit the time that kids spend playing outdoors, exercising or socialising with family and friends, the amount of homework should be decreased. Nature soothes the soul; therefore, governments should ensure that cities are saturated with trees, bushes, shrubs and grass.

Governments should aim to prevent extreme inequality arising in society and, if it exists already, work to reduce it. People will live in poverty and hardship without resentment if all are living under these conditions. However, if the resources of a state are mostly going to one sector of society, allowing them to live luxuriously, while the remainder receive very little, resentment will arise. Resentment can lead to friction and then to rebellion. It should be in the interests of the government to spread the resources of the state fairly across the populace – yet so many fail to do this. Greed, self-interest and a lack of empathy for, or hatred of, others characterise many leaders and governments.

However, it is not just in dictatorships and one-party states that inequality flourishes, it also occurs in democracies – some democracies are more equal than others. If 80 per cent of the wealth in a country is owned by 20 per cent of the people, this is inequality. If the chief executive officer of a company has a salary that is 20, 50 or 100 times greater than that of the average worker in the company, this is inequality. If the children of people who live in a rich neighbourhood have access to better education facilities than the children of those that live in poor neighbourhoods, this is inequality. If everyone in a society has, when needed, quick access to quality medical care that is either free or readily affordable, this is equality. However, if medical care is horrendously expensive, or dependent on prior approval of a profit-driven private health insurance fund that denies approval whenever possible, this is inequality. A rich society is not a great society if death is caused by medical care being withheld because people do not have health insurance or because their health insurance company finds a reason not to pay. National, government-funded health schemes are about caring for citizens, which is what governments should be doing. People covered by such schemes experience much less stress than people who are not.

People can make decisions by a rational, deliberative process in which they logically assess and consider all the facts at hand. They can also make decisions based on more emotional factors such as instinctive or intuitive feelings, ideology and values (e.g. cultural and religious) that are important to them. These latter decisions are more open to evolved biases and can lead to poor outcomes if relied on uncritically. People differ in the extent to which they use one or other of the decision-making processes. Politicians who mostly use the evidence-based, logic process, and take advice from people and organisations that use it, usually make better decisions than those who do not. Politicians receive much non-objective, emotion-based advice and criticism. When this occurs, they should always recognise it for what it is. Most societies contain a number of prominent individuals whose views, at least on some subjects, appear to be entirely emotion based. These people can be dangerous, especially if they are actually in government. Their views, often characterised by irrationality and non-science, can lead to unsound decisions.

Leaders and governments come in two flavours: self and non-self. Self-orientated leaders and governments use the resources of the state solely to benefit themselves and their supporters and to keep themselves in office. In the twenty-first century, such leaders and governments should be extinct. Unfortunately, there are still too many around. Finding a way to make them extinct without major upheavals and bloodshed is a difficult task. Non-self governments (usually found in democracies) use most of the resources of the state to improve the welfare of all their citizens. Of course, it would be ideal if 100 per cent of the resources were used for this purpose, but, given human nature, it is likely that at least some will be used, either directly or indirectly, to keep the incumbents in office. Good governments not only direct most of the state resources to improving the welfare of their citizens, but they do this wisely and efficiently. Doing it wisely requires a good knowledge of human biology, the workings of society and practical economics. Doing it efficiently requires a trained, educated and established public service.

11

SOCIETY

Most people live as members of a large society. The way society is structured, organised and governed influences the well-being of individuals. When there is unrest in a society, a frequent cause is injustice, generated by unequal access to such things as material goods (including, sometimes, food), education and opportunities for advancement, or by unequal application of the laws of the society. Although absolute equality is not possible or desirable (there needs to be some incentive and reward for hard work, creativeness and special skills), care should be taken that the disparity does not become too great. This needs constant vigilance because those that are most well off are usually in positions of authority and, quite frequently, will seek to make changes (often small and subtle, and sometimes made unconsciously) that benefit themselves, thereby increasing inequality. Inequality associated with a recognised group within society (e.g. women or an ethnic or religious minority) can be particularly troublesome.

How, then, to create and maintain an equal society? Here, democracy would appear to be critical, at least for large societies, since history shows that benevolent dictators, monarchs and juntas are rare.

However, it must be a healthy democracy. The characteristics of a healthy democracy are:

1. Every adult has the right to vote.
2. Voting is by secret ballot.
3. Each vote is of equal (or approximately equal) value.
4. There is no tampering with electoral rolls.
5. There is no tampering with votes (possible in many ways).
6. If elections are not held at fixed times, several weeks' (at least) notice of an election is given. Elections held at short notice (e.g. one week) obviously disadvantage non-government parties and candidates.
7. There are no restrictions on individuals or parties standing for election.
8. The selection of candidates by political parties is open and democratic.
9. All candidates and parties standing for election have equal opportunity and access to resources to get their message to the voters.
10. Voters are knowledgeable and sophisticated.

An understanding by voters of society and its problems and how these might be overcome may mean that the candidate offering the biggest barrel of pork may not be elected. Voters are more likely to be knowledgeable and sophisticated if they have received a good education and if media and information sources are numerous, and their content is not manipulated or controlled (i.e. there should be no information management by government), so that all shades of opinion are presented to the people. Discussion in the media should be constant and ongoing, not just in the weeks prior to an election. Accurate information about candidates is also more likely when media outlets are diverse and uncontrolled.

11. Government advertising is regulated by guidelines that only allow advertising when new regulations require a new behaviour by some or all of the citizens about which they need to be informed. Advertising promoting health and safety is also acceptable. Without such guidelines, taxpayer-funded government advertising, especially prior to an election, can be abused to benefit the government.

12. All donations to political parties are, by law, disclosed, except for small donations below

a specified amount. Likewise, non-monetary aid and assistance is declared.

13. Voting is compulsory. With voluntary voting, the well-off citizen is more likely to vote than the poor citizen. Consequently, politicians are likely to make promises that benefit the well-off voter to woo their vote. The result is increased inequality in society. If the poor vote, politicians are more likely to address their needs.

Once a government is fairly elected, some further requirements for a healthy democracy are:

1. A free, diverse and probing media.

2. People or groups outside government, with opinions that differ from those of the government, being able to express those opinions publicly.

3. A free flow of facts and information, both from the government to the people and from specialists in the community to the people. Governments almost universally seek to suppress or distort facts and information that are inconsistent with government policy or that might embarrass them. Whistleblowers that reveal corruption and inefficiencies in government or society should be lauded and protected from penalties. Freedom of information

legislation that has teeth and is not subverted by the government in one way or another is also important.

4. A strong, cohesive opposition party in parliament that constantly questions the government and offers an alternative viewpoint.

5. Government appointees to high courts, commissions, regulatory bodies, non-government organisations and other like bodies are chosen on merit, not on their allegiance to the government, or because of their like-mindedness to those in government or because they have previously donated or contributed to the government party in some way. Ideally, all positions in such organisations should be advertised and appointments made by an independent commission (as does occur in some countries).

6. Those in government are accountable to the public for their decisions and actions. Government members should not surround themselves with large numbers of advisors outside of the public service who, although paid from the public purse, are not accountable to the public or subject to parliamentary scrutiny.

7. Some authority outside of, or independent

of, the government is able to provide some check on the actions of the government. An independent upper house of government can do this at one level. In addition, an independent judiciary with power to modify or strike out government legislation deemed incompatible with basic human rights, freedoms or sound environmental principles is essential. Here it should be noted that "the only thing that stands between the ordinary citizen and tyranny is an independent judiciary". An ombudsman can also provide feedback to the government if legislation is having negative or unintended effects, which, hopefully, would lead to changes in the legislation.

Stress, unrest and ill health can also be generated by laws, customs, values or codes of behaviour (set by the state, or other organisations such as religious bodies or schools) that are incompatible with human nature, needs or environmental circumstances, or that promote, allow or do not act against detrimental activities. Examples include:

- Child prostitution and forced adult prostitution.
- Child soldiers.
- Slavery, bonded labour and child labour.
- Female circumcision.

- Forced and early marriage (usually involving women).

- Marriages in which the customary rights of one partner (usually the husband) greatly exceed the rights of the other partner.

- Laws that are antagonistic to gay individuals or that do not recognise same sex partnerships or that afford such partnerships fewer or lesser rights than heterosexual partnerships.

- Circumstances in which individuals feel powerless because all the important decisions concerning their lives are made by others.

- Banning condoms, which leaves abstinence as the only way to avoid venereal disease and the AIDS virus for those that are not in a long-term monogamous relationship.

- Requiring women to have their whole body completely covered by clothing can lead to vitamin D deficiency due to inadequate exposure of the skin to sunlight if there is insufficient vitamin D in the diet.

- Allowing people to work in dangerous or unhealthy jobs because making the jobs safe would reduce profits.

- Requiring or expecting people to work excessively long hours.

- Allowing the promotion or advertising of unhealthy products or behaviour (e.g. tobacco, "children's" food with high fat, salt or sugar content, using milk formula powders instead of breast milk).

- Creating a society in which, for economic reasons, it is difficult for many women to have children at the optimum age and for a woman or her husband to give up paid work to care for the children, including, for women, being able to breastfeed a baby for an extended period (six to 12 months or more) after birth.

- A justice system that largely relies on confessions obtained by the police to convict alleged criminals.

- Corrupt police and government officials who show no concern for justice and fairness and use their position for personal gain.

- Divorce laws that frequently result in one partner and his or her children never seeing each other again because the partner denied custody is usually given no access rights.

- Government-imposed mandatory sentences for certain misdemeanours or crimes, regardless of circumstances.

- Allowing activities that cause major environmental damage for the immediate economic benefit of a few, which leaves the majority of the people to suffer the long-term consequences.

- Requiring children to sit still and be quiet for long periods.

12

CRIME AND PUNISHMENT

Peter and Paul, both in their late twenties. Peter is easygoing, considerate of others, never violent and a caring husband and father. Paul is antisocial and liable to bouts of uncontrolled rage that often result in aggression and violence. Paul has had these characteristics since childhood. He is in jail because of them.

Looking at Paul, Peter might say, "There, but for the grace of God, go I". However, if Peter were a biologist, he might instead say, "There, but for the genes I received at conception, the environment that I was exposed to prior to birth and in childhood and, perhaps, to chance factors affecting gene activity settings, go I".

Peter, the biologist, could very well be right. Brain scans and other studies have revealed differences between "normal" and chronically angry and aggressive people. Several factors may be involved. One involves the prefrontal cortex, the part of the brain responsible for considered and controlled actions and behaviour.

In chronically angry individuals, the prefrontal cortex is often smaller and, in anger-inducing situations, it is activated far less than in normal people, presumably resulting in a reduced ability to control rage. Another factor is serotonin, a mood stabiliser and behaviour inhibitor that can decrease the firing rate of neurons. Low serotonin levels can predispose individuals to be antisocial and aggressive (especially in combination with high dopamine levels).

People vary in their predisposition to antisocial behaviour and violence. Studies have shown that about half of this variability has a genetic basis, and a few specific gene variants that influence violent behaviour have been identified. However, nurture (the environment) is also important. For example, on the island of Mauritius, a group of children, at age three, were provided with extra nutrition, exercise and intellectual enrichment for two years. Eighteen years later, these individuals showed 35 per cent less criminal behaviour compared with individuals in a control group who had not received the nurturing boost. A second example: studies have found that individuals with low serotonin levels who were maltreated as children are more likely to be antisocial and aggressive than low serotonin individuals brought up in a loving, nurturing environment. Brains are designed to change and build up pathways in response to experience. This may be an example.

Thus, it is probable that, in Paul's case, his hostile and aggressive nature is a consequence of genes + environment (womb and childhood experiences) + chance. These are factors over which Paul had no control. Yet, in many countries, the law is based on the assumption that people have free will and are therefore responsible for their behaviour. This is why Paul is in jail.

How should a "civilised" society handle people like Paul? How should a "civilised" society handle criminals in general if we recognise that genes + childhood environment have a significant influence on a person's character?

One possible approach is to make a judgement first about the extent to which the criminal behaviour is the result of factors such as the structure and regulation of the brain and childhood experiences, which it is difficult for the individual to override or control, rather than a deliberate act of free will. At one end of the spectrum would be people who are violent or commit criminal acts because of chromosome abnormalities and/or brain abnormalities and/or mistreatment as a child. In the middle of the spectrum might be people who are addicted to drugs or gambling and steal to support their habit. These might be followed by individuals who commit one-off, spur-of-the-moment criminal acts. At the other end of the spectrum would be those involved in robberies planned weeks or months in advance, those involved in carefully orchestrated fraud and those involved in organised crime that is a business. The penalties imposed by a court might then reflect the amount of free will involved in the criminal act. In many societies in which laws have "evolved" with the times, this already occurs to a fair degree.

However, the predetermined-versus-free-will aspect of a crime is not the only determinant of the nature of the penalty. In addition to the severity of the crime, several other elements can have an influence. One is the deterrent aspect. Sometimes penalties are imposed not just to punish the offender, but to deter others from carrying out similar crimes. Whether it is reasonable to over punish one individual in an attempt to protect society by deterring others from committing a particular crime is a matter for debate. The first question to answer is whether unusually severe penalties do act as a deterrent. They may for coldly calculated deliberate crimes but probably do not for crimes of passion committed by people in a state of anger. It is worth noting here that the best deterrent to deliberate crime is a high probability of being caught, not an excessively severe penalty if caught.

Another factor influencing the nature of a penalty is the probability that an offender will reoffend. In general, the more an individual continues to commit crimes despite previous convictions, the more appropriate a prison sentence becomes. In the case above, Paul may not be responsible for his violence, but if his bouts of uncontrolled anger regularly result in people being injured, society does have a right to protect itself by placing Paul in a facility that denies him access to the public. Ideally, such a facility would not be a prison, but a less severe confinement situation with a strong emphasis on treatment, for drugs and behaviour therapy can successfully control violent behaviour in some people.

Finally, three additional factors can and should influence the nature of a penalty. The first is whether the crime involved a threat to life or a chance of injury: $100 stolen from the wallet of a man threatened with a gun or knife is a more serious crime than $100 stolen from a wallet left on a work desk. The second factor is the effect that a particular penalty might have on innocent third parties. A judge might legitimately seek to avoid a prison sentence for a sole parent if such a sentence is likely to cause stress or harm to a dependent child or children. The third factor is whether there was a victim associated with the crime or whether the crime was victimless. Harsh penalties for victimless crimes such as protesting a government law or breaking a religious decree would seem unwarranted. Other crimes such as growing a few cannabis plants for personal use would also appear to be victimless but may not be so if use of the cannabis contributes to an accident in which people are injured or to children receiving less care than otherwise (alcohol use is similar). For some crimes, the victim is the government or society in general: tax fraud and vandalism of community assets are examples. Thus, there are shades of grey in the extent to which a crime has a victim.

Therefore, judges need to weigh up multiple factors when deciding on a penalty for a crime. The list includes:

- Degree of free will involved.
- Severity of crime.
- Deterrent effect.
- Probability of reoffending.
- Was there a threat of physical harm to victim(s)?
- Effect of penalty on innocent third parties.
- Was there a victim?

Once an assessment of these factors has been made, does a judge give equal weighting to each, or give some factors more weight than others? Clearly, a conscientious judge has much to consider when deciding on an appropriate penalty. The penalty should be tailor-made to each individual offender and the circumstances of the case. Fixed mandatory sentences imposed by governments do not achieve this.

The selection of judges is obviously important. Good governments will appoint individuals who not only have a good knowledge of the law but also have appropriate personal qualities. These might include having personal integrity, being well-rounded, being in touch with society and having the ability to make rational assessments based on the facts at hand.

Crime committed by individuals or small groups of individuals will always be present; however, although distressing to the victims, such crime is not a fundamental threat to society provided that the proportion of such people in a society is kept low by a well-trained, well-equipped and adequately staffed police force.

However, fundamental threats to society do arise if crime and corruption become systemic in the power structures of society. The worst case (the ultimate cancer) is when those in government, or the ruling elite, are corrupt, since this can lead, with time, to corruption of those managing government funds and the economy, those in the public service, the judiciary, the police and those in charge of the armed forces.

Lower-level corruption, usually for monetary gain, can also seriously debilitate a society if it becomes widespread: examples include use of public monies or assets for personal gain and bribery of public servants, judges and the police (or their direct participation in criminal activities). Other cancers in a society are large, well-organised bodies whose activities benefit a few at the expense of the majority, such as the mafia, drug cartels, groups of elite businesspeople arranging monopolies, fixing prices or corruptly acquiring government contracts, grants or subsidies and exploitative unions.

It is vital to the well-being of society that cancers such as those outlined above do not become entrenched, since, if they do, they become very difficult to eliminate. Systems to identify such cancers need to be always in place and constantly refreshed. Separate and independent power sources within a society, a free and probing press and a positive and supportive approach to whistleblowers are all elements that will aid this quest. An independent ombudsman and a permanent, independent commission against corruption, misconduct and crime, with the power to initiate investigations into all agencies of power and areas of human activity in a society, should be standard in all large societies. Such bodies would form a solid legal foundation and backup to the forward scouts:

complaints mechanisms, honest and concerned colleagues, auditors, external review agencies, criminal justice mechanisms and parliamentary enquiries. There will almost always be some who are tempted when they have control over large sums of money, can influence the awarding of contracts, receive valuable information or are in a position to make decisions capable of benefiting or hurting important interests. In the longer term, reducing the value that many societies currently put on having a great deal of material goods may also contribute in this regard. So too may positive enrichment of early childhood experiences. Basic integrity and honesty (or lack of it) may already be fixed in an individual by age seven. The more positives that a society can turn out at this age, the better off it will be in the longer run.

13

RELIGION, GODS AND SPIRIT ANCESTORS

Twelve thousand years ago, all humans lived in small tribal groups dispersed over six continents. Apparently most, if not all, of these groups had developed a spiritual element to their lives, which often included a system of one or more gods or spirit ancestors, usually with supernatural powers. Why did a belief in higher beings arise almost universally prior to civilisation? Two main hypotheses have been put forward. The first proposes that there were benefits to be obtained from a belief in a superbeing or beings – benefits that could apply to individuals and/or to the group/society in which they lived. What might such benefits be?

It seems likely that the spiritual element arose and superbeings were conceived when the brains of our ancestors evolved to a stage that enabled higher levels of awareness, permitted imagination and made it possible for questions about how and why to be posed. For example, when our ancestors became aware that the quality of their lives was dependent on environmental factors (e.g. rain, abundance of prey species, wildfire), that healthy people can suddenly get sick (and perhaps die) for no obvious reason and that a steady production of children (good fertility) was necessary for their own well-being in old age and for the well-being and defence of their tribe and society. When they began to wonder about the sun, moon, stars, thunder and lightning and the origins of the land, life and the first human beings. When they developed a sense that there was more to a human being than just the material body – in other words, when the idea that human beings had souls was conceived. When they became aware that death comes to everyone. When they felt the need for life to have a purpose – that there was more to life than just eating, reproducing and dying.

By creating superbeings with superpowers our ancestors were no longer powerless. Offerings, tributes and sacrifices, along with pleas and prayers, could be made to the appropriate superbeing to overcome or prevent natural disasters, sickness and low fertility. Entities in the heavens, the origin of the world and the source of life upon it could be attributed to one or more superbeings and their creative abilities. Fear of death was reduced either by a belief in an afterlife in the heavens, often in association with a god or gods, or by a belief in reincarnation in another life on Earth. In some cases, purpose was given to life because humans were now agents in god's scheme for the universe.

Thus to the "aware" human being, it is likely that religion, gods and spirit ancestors reduced the sense of helplessness in the face of nature and the fear of death, and satisfied a need for structure and purpose in the world, while providing a framework in which the existence of a soul could readily be incorporated.

At the group level, religion could provide a source of beliefs, laws, customs and morals for regulating the behaviour of individuals. This may have enabled groups to function better. Religion may also have acted as a cohesive force that facilitated the formation of larger cooperative groups. Such groups would likely be more successful in competition for resources. Thus, evolution may have favoured individuals with minds capable of accepting religion because such individuals formed better-functioning and larger groups.

The second hypothesis for the development of a belief in higher beings is that such a belief does not confer benefits (as outlined above) but is a by-product of brains that have evolved to accept instruction from authoritative individuals (see, for example, *The God Delusion* by Richard Dawkins). This hypothesis notes that a unique feature of the human species is the long time it takes to reach adulthood, a characteristic that is likely to have evolved because humans have a great deal to learn before they reach maturity. Much of this learning is acquired from authoritative and skilled adults in the child's tribe or society. As a consequence, hypothesis 2 argues that our brains have evolved to accept, and perhaps to seek, the words of authoritative individuals because this facilitates the learning process, and that, as a by-product of this evolution, adult humans are preconditioned to accept the existence of authoritative higher beings and to follow any teachings or instructions attributed to them. Any such preconditioning could, of course, be exploited by manipulative individuals seeking some personal benefit such as increased power.

The two hypotheses outlined above are not alternatives to each other. Both – or elements of both – may be true.

If gods and religion did arise for some or all of the reasons outlined above, is there still a need for "God" in the current scientific age? For many people, the answer is clearly "yes" since, given a choice, they have chosen to belong to a religion and to believe in the existence of a god. Today, the principal reasons for this choice are probably to satisfy a need for a spiritual element to life, a need for life to have a purpose and a sense of direction, and a need to feel that death is not the end of everything. The need to provide an explanation of the physical world through god(s) is probably not as great as it was for our early ancestors, because science can now largely satisfy this need for most people.

However, while many people do choose to believe in a god and to belong to a religion, many others choose not to. Clearly, people differ in their spiritual needs and in their need for a god. Societies that recognise these differences and allow their members to join – or not to join – a religion are likely to satisfy the majority of their members best. Societies that ban all religions, or that insist that all members belong to one particular religion, are likely to generate stress and frustration in a significant proportion of their members.

One additional point should be noted here. A strong case can be made for *not* thrusting religious dogma on young children because most are not capable of critically assessing what they are told and it can cause them much stress and trauma. An extreme example (reported by Richard Dawkins in his book *The God Delusion*) is that of a seven-year-old girl of Catholic parents whose best friend, a seven-year-old girl of Protestant parents, died. The Catholic girl suffered immense trauma over an extended period of

time because she was told (and believed) that her
friend, being Protestant, would not be in heaven but
would be suffering, and would suffer for ever, in the
fires of hell. Less dramatically, individuals who have
been force-fed religious dogma as children sometimes suffer anxiety and stress if, as adults, they decide that they can no longer accept some or all of the
religious teachings drummed into them during their
childhood days.

14

Ecosystem Management

Food from the Land

Governments have a responsibility to look to the well-being of future generations, not just the present generation. This means maintaining the carrying capacity of the environment. It means living off the interest provided by the environment and not mining its capital or degrading it so that its capacity to produce interest is reduced. Since humans have been mining and degrading the environment for thousands of years, governments also now have a responsibility (and urgent need) to start repairing it.

We can care for the environment for largely altruistic reasons (e.g. to prevent plants and animals from becoming extinct) or for reasons of self-interest. Let's go for self-interest. The biggest item on the self-interest list is food. Already, with seven billion people in the world, one billion do not get enough food and two billion have inadequate food quality. With an additional two billion expected in the next three decades, together with likely supply and price pressures on the inputs required for food production, producing enough food to feed everyone adequately is going to be difficult. Well-researched books that detail the problems are available, such as *The Coming Famine: The Global Food Crisis and What We Can Do to Avoid It* by Julian Cribb. Such books should be required reading for every politician and every member of government. After all, it is in their own interest to look to food security. Voters might be unhappy when unemployment rises and petrol prices go up, but when food prices double and shortages start to appear they can get extremely angry. A Spanish proverb states "Civilisation and anarchy are only seven meals apart".

So to food. Here we owe everything to photosynthetic organisms. We should love them dearly. All human and most animal and fungal life is absolutely dependent on them.

Photosynthetic organisms – plants, algae, both large (seaweeds) and small (phytoplankton) and some bacteria – are miracle workers. They have the unique capacity to take carbon dioxide and water molecules and, using energy from sunlight, turn them into sugar and oxygen molecules. They then use the sugar molecules, and the energy captured in their chemical bonds, together with nitrates, phosphates, sulphates and the atoms of 11 or so other elements taken from the soil or surrounding water to synthesise all the other types of organic molecules, for example, starch, proteins, oils, vitamins and DNA. Thus, photosynthetic organisms are the primary source of all the food we eat, the oxygen we breathe, fibre (cotton, linen, jute and hemp), timber, rubber and many other products used in industry. Long-term, sustainable production from these organisms should be a high priority of every government.

The bulk of our food comes from plants. Plants need land on which to grow, water, fertilisers and a suitable climate (temperature and light). If there are shortages of any of these factors and/or they are only available in a suboptimum state, food production will be reduced. As documented by Julian Cribb (see above), food production is already being constrained by each of these factors, and these constraints have the potential to increase markedly in the near future unless governments become serious about tackling them.

Land

The amount of land available for agriculture, and the quality of that land, are major determinants of plant-based food production. Clearing of jungle and drainage of peat land, mainly in South America and South-East Asia, are currently making additional land available. However, these operations have a cost: they release large amounts of greenhouse gases and cause species and biodiversity loss. In an ideal world, such operations would be halted. Some have been but, given the population, economic and political pressures in the countries involved, these activities will almost certainly continue to some extent. Some additional land may also become available if the warming associated with increased levels of greenhouse gases in the atmosphere allows agriculture to extend to higher latitudes in the Northern Hemisphere. However, this gain will almost certainly be offset by the loss of land resulting from rising sea levels that will also accompany global warming. This land loss will be particularly marked in delta areas, which are usually extremely fertile. Reduced silt deposition by rivers on delta regions due to the construction of dams is also contributing to delta loss. Also on the debit side, large areas of good quality agricultural land are being lost as cities constantly expand and industrial activity increases due to an ever-increasing population. Built-up areas, most of which are on good farmland, already occupy five million square kilometres, and in the United States alone, more than a million acres of agricultural land are taken over for other uses each year.

We have reached the stage at which more people

means less land for food production – this cannot go on forever.

Land quality, which relates to the yielding capacity of the land, has also suffered. It has been estimated that approximately 25 per cent of the world's land surface has been degraded to some extent. The causes of this degradation are soil loss due to erosion by wind and water, salinisation, loss of fertility, problems with the physical structure of the soil and industrial pollution. This degradation does not just affect croplands, but also forests and rangelands. Importantly, this degradation can be arrested and even reversed by the right sort of farming practices.

It should be an absolute priority of all governments to maintain and improve land quality. Unfortunately, with many governments, it is not. In many areas, the degradation is continuing. It is future generations that will suffer the consequences.

Water

In areas or seasons of low rainfall, irrigation will boost production. In theory, more irrigation will give more food – and thus, problem solved. In practice, 70 per cent of the Earth's readily available freshwater is already used in irrigation, and the amount available for this purpose in the future is likely to decline. This decline will occur because of an ever-increasing urban demand for water, along with a recognition that too much water is being taken from certain rivers and that some of it needs to be returned for the health of those rivers. In addition, a great deal of irrigation water comes from groundwater aquifers and many of these are being depleted due to overexploitation. The main scope for improvement here is to prevent water wastage by installing pipes to replace open canals and channels, which lose water through seepage and evaporation. In some situations, water can also be used more efficiently by using drip irrigation in place of sprinklers.

Fertilisers

Plant nutrients, principally nitrogen, phosphorus and potassium, are lost from the soil whenever a crop is harvested, animals sent to an abattoir or timber harvested. Unless the soil is exceptionally fertile, these elements need to be replaced. For most large-scale agriculture operations, this entails adding chemical fertilisers. These fertilisers are of critical importance because it has been estimated that, without them, world food production would be reduced by 50 per cent. Given this, will supplies continue to be available in the future?

Nitrogen fertiliser is manufactured – currently at the rate of over 120 million tonnes a year – from natural gas. Supplies are not likely to be limited in the foreseeable future. Phosphorus fertiliser comes from rock phosphate mines, principally in China and Morocco/Western Sahara, and in smaller amounts from South Africa and the United States. Based on one assessment, these mines have less than 80 years' supply remaining. Although other phosphate sources are available, most of these are of poorer quality. Potassium fertiliser (potash) comes mainly from mines in Canada, Russia, Belarus, China and Germany. Based on current usage, the known reserves will last about 300 years. Thus, with regard to fertiliser availability in the future, phosphorus will be the problem. Food shortages due to a lack of phosphate could occur in the lifetimes of present-day children.

The large-scale use of chemical fertilisers, however, has negative effects on the environment. The manufacture of nitrogen fertiliser requires large quantities of fossil fuels and generates large amounts of greenhouse gases. Yet, a bigger problem is that up to 50 per cent of these fertilisers leak into freshwater rivers, lakes and dams and then into the sea. In these bodies of water, they often combine with nutrients from other sources such as sewerage, urban stormwater, soil erosion and leaky landfills to produce a nutrient broth. These broths can feed blooms of algae, which, when they decompose, can produce oxygen-deficient dead zones. These are discussed in more detail below.

In the future, as nutrient shortages develop, greater efforts will be made to prevent nutrient loss, to capture any that do escape and to reuse those that have entered the food chain by recycling all plant and animal products and human waste, especially sewerage. Currently, in many places, little recycling is carried out. It would make sense to increase our efforts now.

Climate

Most plant species are adapted to a particular environment. Likewise, crop varieties are bred or selected for a specific environment. Therefore, if one environmental factor changes, the losses are likely to be greater than the gains. A key environmental factor that *is* changing is climate as increasing levels of greenhouse gases in the atmosphere cause temperatures to rise (see Chapter 17). The deleterious effects can be general, such as a change in the rainfall pattern or stronger storms and cyclones bringing higher winds and more flooding rains – or the effects can be specific, such as plants failing to set seed or fruit due to high temperatures at flowering time or failing to flower because they have not received the extended period of cold that is required to induce flowering. Benefits could also be general, such as allowing agriculture to extend into higher latitudes in the Northern Hemisphere, or specific, such as less yield loss in wheat in some areas due to fewer frosts at flowering time (which prevent seed set). Pests and diseases of plants are also likely to be affected by climate change in unpredictable ways.

Loss and wastage

Currently huge losses of food – more than one-third – occur worldwide at all stages of the food cycle. During crop growth, pests, diseases and weeds commonly cause significant yield losses. After harvest, if storage conditions are inadequate, fruit and vegetables can rot and grain can be attacked by weevils. Perfectly sound fruit and vegetables may be thrown out for cosmetic reasons such as surface blemishes or because they are the wrong size or shape. And consumers, particularly in affluent countries, frequently throw away significant amounts of the final food product because they prepare more than can be consumed or because the food is not used before the use-by date.

Preventing these losses has great potential to increase food supply.

Pests and diseases can often be controlled by sprays, but these can sometimes have deleterious side effects. Alternative approaches include incorporating into the crop variety genes that confer in-built resistance to the pest or pathogen or, for insect pests, using baits, pheromones and natural predators to reduce their numbers: these approaches usually only become possible after extensive scientific study. Postharvest losses can be prevented by upgrading storage facilities, making greater use of refrigeration, storing grain in insect-proof and gas-tight silos and improving transport systems. Consumer wastage might be reduced by education, invoking a sense of shame, and by higher prices.

There are good returns to be made from investments that reduce loss and wastage. In particular, good returns can come when scientists find or develop genes that provide in-built resistance to pests and diseases or identify and employ natural predators of pest insects. Governments should take note.

15

Ecosystem Management

Food from the Sea

The principal source of high-quality animal protein for one billion people is fish from the sea. To maintain this important food resource, we need to avoid overfishing and ensure that we do not alter the environment in the sea in ways that adversely affect fish reproduction and growth. On both counts, we score poorly.

We have overfished many fish species: almost one in three fisheries has collapsed or is in the process of collapsing. Collapses commonly occur when high levels of fishing continue even when it is clear that fish numbers are in sharp decline, due to short-term greed and governments failing to step in. Overfishing is also likely to occur in coastal areas near countries where poverty and hunger are rife, when impoverished governments sell fishing rights to foreign fishing fleets for instant cash, when nations allow pirate trawlers to use their ports and in open oceans where fish catches are regulated by regional fisheries

management organisations in which political appointees commonly ignore scientific advice and, instead,
pursue (short-term) national interests at the expense
of the long-term well-being of the fishery. The use of
very large trawlers equipped with giant nets and sophisticated fish-locating equipment facilitates overfishing. More positively, often, but not always, fisheries can recover if catches are reduced or stopped
entirely, marine reserves established and nursery areas protected. Success will often depend on a good,
science-based knowledge of the life history and ecol-
ogy of the fish species concerned.

In the long run, however, the many environmental changes being wrought by human activities
may do the most harm. Mangroves, coastal seagrass
plains and coral reefs provide nurseries and habitat
for many fish species. All are under attack. Around
the world, large areas of mangroves have been, and
continue to be, removed for prawn farms and other
"development" purposes. Seagrass is often killed or
severely affected by floodwaters carrying herbicides,
fertilisers and large amounts of sediment from agricultural land. Coral reefs are disappearing at an
alarming rate at many places around the world. A
study of 214 sites over a 27-year period (1985–2012)
of the 2,000-kilometre long Great Barrier Reef along
the eastern coast of Australia recorded a 50 per cent

loss in coral cover. Forty-eight per cent of the loss was attributed to damage caused by tropical cyclones, 42 per cent to outbreaks of the crown-of-thorns starfish, which eats the polyps inside the coral skeleton, and 10 per cent to coral bleaching events, in which corals lose their algae partners due to overly-warm sea temperatures. Human activities likely contributed to all these losses. Global warming, caused by increased greenhouse gas emissions, has also warmed the sea (up by 2° C in some places). Warmer seas likely feed more energy into cyclones, making them more intense, which in turn can lead to greater coral loss. Coral bleaching events are also likely to occur more frequently as seas warm. Possibly increased by more intense cyclones, floodwaters carrying fertilisers into the ocean are thought to be responsible for the crown-of-thorns outbreaks. The fertiliser promotes algal growth, which is a food source for the crown-of-thorns larvae and thus enables large numbers of these to survive. In some parts of the world, coral reefs are also being directly destroyed when explosives or cyanide poisoning are used to catch fish.

Besides the loss of mangrove, seagrass and coral reef habitats, human activity is responsible for several other changes to the sea environment that either now negatively affect fish numbers or will do so in the future.

In addition to those influences noted above, warmer seas will allow warm-water fish to migrate to areas that were previously too cold for them. This is already taking place. As a consequence, fish adapted to cold water may be negatively affected due to increased competition and/or because there is less of the cold-water habitat to which they are adapted.

The higher carbon dioxide level in the atmosphere – up from 280 parts per million (ppm) 200 years ago to around 400 ppm today – not only contributes to global warming but also makes the seas more acid. This occurs because around 25 per cent of the extra carbon dioxide released by human activities ends up dissolved in seawater, where it forms acid ions. Seawater currently contains 30 per cent more acid ions than it did a century ago, and the number is steadily increasing. As seawater acidifies, the concentration of carbonate ions, a constituent of calcium carbonate, declines. Declining concentrations of carbonate ions impair the ability of calcifying organisms such as corals, clams, snails, urchins and some calcareous algae to build their protective shells and skeletons. Further, if the concentration of carbonate ions falls below a certain level, the calcium carbonate already in the shells of marine organisms starts to dissolve. Although the current acidity levels do not appear to have caused a significant problem, this is a major concern for the future because the ocean will continue to become more acidic. That shells can actually dissolve is not just theory. There is a region in the southern Atlantic Ocean that is more acidic than the general ocean due to an upwelling of deep, CO_2-enriched water. Shells of a small planktonic mollusc collected from this site showed signs of dissolution along their entire length. However, although it has not been tested, these molluscs may still have been producing new shell material, since a related species has been shown to be capable of this under similar conditions of acidity. Because these small molluscs can occur in large numbers and are important food sources for zooplankton, herring, salmon, seabirds and whales, their loss or decline could lead to a major collapse of some fish populations.

Humans produce a great deal of chemicals (currently over 80,000 different kinds amounting to 30 million tonnes a year), a great deal of fertiliser and a great deal of waste from urban, industrial and mining sources. Significant amounts of these materials end up in the sea. Since many of the chemicals and waste materials are toxic, and some are known or suspected to be a cause of cancer, mutations and birth defects, their presence in the sea is likely to have a negative influence on the life forms living there. Of particular concern are fertilisers: it has been estimated that around half of the world's annual fertiliser use (120 million tonnes of nitrogen and nine million tonnes of phosphorus) escape into the world's rivers, lakes and oceans yearly. In the oceans, these fertilisers contribute to algae blooms, which, when they die and subsequently decay, can produce dead zones that are largely devoid of oxygen. Over 400 dead zones were reported in 2012, some of which were huge, such as the one that covered 22,000 square kilometres at the mouth of the Mississippi River. Fish cannot live in dead zones – and this is not good for people who rely on fish as their prime protein source.

The wild fish harvest from the oceans has been in decline since 1997, despite the use of larger fishing vessels with bigger nets and sophisticated technology. The steps required to allow fisheries to recover are known but, given that in many places short-term commercial interests with government connivance reign supreme and that in some cases agreement between different governments is required, there cannot be a lot of confidence that the steps will be carried out. A World Bank report in 2009 calculated that the major fish stocks of the world would produce 40 per cent more if we fished them less for a while. Surely stopping or reducing catches for a number of years to allow a fishery to recover so that a long-term sustainable catch can be achieved, rather than losing the fishery completely, makes simple sense. Those affected by loss of income during the recovery years would need to be compensated. All that is needed is for governments to show some integrity, make the necessary decisions and then enforce those decisions. Governments that do nothing should be condemned, and condemned again. Future generations will not thank them.

16

Ecosystem Management

Nightmare Scenarios

Nightmare scenarios can be fun – especially in the movies. Dreaming them up can be fun, provided that the probability of them actually occurring is infinitesimally small or their timing is set a long way into the future. Unfortunately, some nightmare scenarios have appeared on the horizon in recent times whose probability of occurring is not infinitesimally small and, if they did occur, could occur within one, two or a few generations. It really is time for governments to sit up, take notice and initiate some serious actions. Unfortunately, most governments are still snoozing.

17

Nightmare Scenario 1
Global Warming and Climate Change

Temperature measurements show that the world has grown hotter over the past 100 years, particularly so over the last 35 years. The rise in temperature is not uniform: areas near the poles have warmed more than those near the equator, and places in the centre of some continents have warmed more than those at the coast. The average near-surface air temperature has increased by around 0.75° C. Seas and oceans have also warmed – the surface of the ocean by about 0.5° C on average. The observation that virtually every glacier in the world is retreating and that sea and land ice in the Arctic is diminishing is also a clear indication that heating is occurring.

So, why is the world growing hotter? Is it because the world has orbited closer to the Sun over the last few decades? No, this has not occurred. Is it because the Sun has grown hotter and is sending more radiation our way? No, satellite measurements since 1979 show that solar output has not significantly increased

since that time, and some measurements even indicate that the Sun has grown slightly cooler since
1960. Is it because, by burning oil, coal and gas, or
producing energy in nuclear reactors, we are releas-
ing heat into the environment that was previously
locked away underground in the form of chemical
energy or locked up in the mass of atomic particles?
Yes, but calculations show that these heat sources
have only contributed a small amount of the heating
that has occurred. Is it because more of the radiation
that reaches the Earth from the Sun is being retained
by the Earth, with less escaping back into space? Yes –
there is no doubt that this is the main reason that the
world is warming.

So, why is this happening? First, some back-
ground. In addition to the main gases of nitrogen
(78%), oxygen (21%) and argon (1%), the atmosphere
contains variable amounts of water vapour and small
amounts of other gases, of which carbon dioxide
(CO_2), methane (CH_4), nitrous oxide (N_2O), ozone
(O_3) and synthetic gases such as chlorofluorocarbons
and hydrofluorocarbons are of particular interest.
Water vapour and all the minor gases just listed have
the capacity to absorb radiation with wavelengths in
the infra-red range. When they do this, they vibrate
faster and become hotter. When these faster-vibrating
molecules collide with other molecules, they make

them vibrate faster, thus heating the whole environment. Because they absorb outgoing infra-red radiation emitted by the Earth that would otherwise be lost to space, these infra-red absorbing molecules increase the Earth's temperature. It has been calculated that, without these gases, the average global temperature would be 18° C below freezing: 32° C cooler than at present. These infra-red absorbing gases, because of their Earth-warming ability, are otherwise known as greenhouse gases.

The incoming radiation from the Sun has wavelengths mostly in the infra-red and visible-light range with a small amount in the ultraviolet (UV) light range. As this radiation passes through the atmosphere, a significant amount of the UV light is absorbed by ozone in the upper atmosphere and some of the infra-red radiation is absorbed by the greenhouse gases. The remainder of the incoming solar radiation will end up hitting something solid – this may be a minute droplet of water in a cloud, a particle in the atmosphere or, commonly, something on the surface of the Earth. When this occurs, part of the Sun's radiation is reflected and part is absorbed by the solid matter. Radiation that is reflected upwards may pass back through the atmosphere and be lost to the Earth. Radiation that is absorbed causes the molecules of the solid matter to vibrate faster, so the solid matter becomes hotter. The more energetic molecules may lose energy by collisions with less energetic molecules and by emitting infra-red radiation. The emitted infra-red radiation, if emitted upwards, may pass through the atmosphere and be lost from the Earth. However, again, some will be absorbed by the greenhouse gas molecules. Therefore, if the number of greenhouse gas molecules in the atmosphere increases, more of the emitted infra-red radiation will be retained in the atmosphere (thereby making it hotter) and less will escape back into space. Moreover, the number of greenhouse gas molecules has increased from pre-industrial times: CO_2 has increased from 280 ppm to around 400 ppm today, methane has doubled to 1.8 ppm and nitrous oxide levels have increased by 20 per cent to 0.325 ppm.

If more of the outgoing infra-red radiation is being trapped by increased amounts of greenhouse gases in the atmosphere, less of this radiation is expected to reach the upper atmosphere (the stratosphere). The stratosphere would therefore be expected to grow colder. If the world were getting hotter due to increased radiation from the Sun, the stratosphere would be expected to grow warmer. The stratosphere has, in fact, grown colder over the past few decades, indicating that increased greenhouse gases are the principal cause of the Earth's warming.

About 80 per cent of the increased amount of CO_2 in the atmosphere has come from the burning of fossil fuels (oil, coal and gas); most of the rest has come from the clearing of forests (which releases CO_2 stored in vegetation and in organic matter in the soil). A small amount has come from industrial processes, including cement making (which releases CO_2 from limestone). Ideally, the world should be moving as quickly as possible to reduce CO_2 emissions from these sources. In fact, although significant resources are being put into renewable energy sources in some countries, annual CO_2 emissions are still increasing and are unlikely to fall in the near future due to an ever-increasing population. In addition, less-developed countries use more energy as they industrialise and energy from fossil fuel sources is mostly cheaper than that from renewable sources.

The world still has huge reserves of coal and large reserves of natural gas. In addition, fracking has made accessible a great deal of oil and gas that was previously unattainable. Significant new reserves of oil and gas may become accessible as the Arctic sea ice disappears. Therefore, CO_2 production is not going to slow down in the near future because of fossil fuel exhaustion. CO_2 production will only slow down if, worldwide, deliberate and large-scale efforts are made to do so.

So, what is the nightmare scenario associated with greenhouse gas increases?

Modelling, together with an examination of past climate change events, suggests that if CO_2 emissions decline sharply from now on so that CO_2 levels peak at 450 ppm (currently around 400 ppm), the temperature increase would be about 2° C above pre-industrial levels. However, annual global emissions are still rising and any significant reduction is not likely to occur in the near future. Given this, there is likely to be a doubling of pre-industrial CO_2 levels later this century, which is predicted to give a long-term warming of 3° C (with an uncertainty range of 2° C to 4.5° C). A tripling of pre-industrial CO_2 would be expected to produce a warming of 4.5° C (range 3° C to 7° C). The problem is that there are additional unknowns because, as the Earth warms, positive feedbacks may kick in that warm the Earth even more.

A direct warming feedback is occurring in the Arctic, where, due to the temperature rise that has already occurred, large areas of the sea that once retained sea ice in summer now usually become open water. This leads to increased heat retention because white sea ice reflects much of the incoming solar radiation, whereas dark seawater absorbs most of it. The same is happening on land, where reflective white snow now melts more often to reveal less-reflective dirty ice.

Additional indirect warming comes from positive feedback factors that are, or may be, adding greenhouse gases to the atmosphere. The average water vapour content in the atmosphere has been increasing at a rate of one to two per cent per decade since the 1980s, when reliable measurements began. Water molecules are a potent greenhouse gas; however, their greenhouse effect may be partially offset if there is increased cloud cover because clouds reflect some solar radiation back to space.

Another positive feedback factor, potentially of huge significance, relates to the massive amount of carbon stored in the ground and oceans of the Earth and the extent to which this might start to be released as the Earth warms. In the past 250 years, humankind has released about 540 billion tonnes of carbon into the atmosphere (one tonne of carbon equates to 3.67 tonnes of CO_2). However, it has been estimated that nearly 1,700 billion tonnes of carbon is currently locked up in frozen soils in the Arctic region. One estimate indicates that thawing as a result of warming over the next 100 years could release 100 billion tonnes of this carbon as CO_2 or methane, leading to an extra warming of 0.25° C and possibly up to 1° C. There are also large deposits of methane clathrates (in which a large amount of methane is trapped within a crystal structure of water molecules forming a solid similar to ice) beneath the Arctic and continental seabeds, which currently represent a largely unknown risk. Large deposits of carbon also exist in tropical peat lands, of which about 30 billion tonnes could be released as CO_2 or methane by drainage or fire. There is also a massive amount of CO_2 dissolved in the world's oceans, particularly in the deep, cold waters of the Southern Ocean. If warmer temperatures cause more of this cold, CO_2-rich water to be brought to the surface (for example, by increased wave action or a change in currents), as the water warmed, CO_2 would be released back into the atmosphere because warm water can hold less dissolved CO_2 than cold water. In addition, as oceans warm, currents carrying warm tropical waters to colder regions may weaken, causing tropical waters to warm even more and therefore release dissolved CO_2. Thus, positive carbon feedbacks could occur from several sources. The extent is hard to quantify. This is a significant area of uncertainty. But what is certain is that the more CO_2 that we release directly into the environment, the greater is the risk that these positive feedback factors will come into play. The danger is that this carbon feedback could lead to a self-perpetuating cycle, such that, even if all human emissions stopped, carbon levels might continue to rise due to carbon released from frozen Arctic soils, tropical peat lands and the oceans, leading to further warming and further carbon releases – a runaway greenhouse effect.

So, the world is definitely on track for further warming: although with wide error margins, a common prediction is a 3° C increase later this century and a possible 4.5° C increase sometime next century. Much of the extra heat trapped by the additional greenhouse gases ends up warming the ocean. It has been estimated that 90 per cent of the extra heat that the Earth has acquired in the past 100 years has gone to warming the top 700 metres of the ocean. This is important because ocean temperatures have a great influence on weather patterns (see below).

What, then, will be the effects of the higher temperatures to come? They are likely to be many and varied.

1. The Earth is a global heat engine. Warm, moist air at the tropics rises. As it does so, it cools and dumps all its moisture. This now dry air moves towards the poles, cooling further along the way. When sufficiently cooled, it sinks back to the Earth's surface. Being so dry, the places to which it sinks tend to be deserts. If the air is hotter to begin with, it will travel further in the upper atmosphere before cooling sufficiently to sink. This may mean that desert regions move to higher latitudes

– thus, the Sahara could move into southern Europe.

2. Weather patterns are likely to change. For example, in the Northern Hemisphere, the polar jetstream, which pushes weather systems around, may be weakening as temperature differences between the tropics and the Arctic fall. The weakened polar jetstream appears to be meandering more and slowing down, so that weather patterns are more likely to get stuck in one place. Weather patterns are generated by patterns of pressure differences, which are greatly influenced by ocean temperatures. As the oceans warm, ocean currents may change, affecting ocean temperatures in different ways in different places – which will likely generate different weather patterns. Already there is evidence of a shift in weather systems towards the Earth's polar regions. For agriculture, this is likely to have more negative than positive effects.

3. Sea levels have risen by about 20 centimetres in the past 150 years. During most of the twentieth century, the increase averaged about 1.7 millimetres per year, but from the early 1990s, this increased to about three millimetres per year. Satellite measurements show

that Greenland is losing ice due to increased surface melt and an increased flow of ice into the ocean and that the rate of this loss has risen markedly since the mid-1990s. In addition, recent estimates show that Antarctica as a whole is losing ice. Thus, increased ice loss has contributed to the higher rate of sea level rise observed in the last 20 years. However, extra water in the ocean from the melting of land ice (and from the pumping out of underground aquifers) is not the major cause of most of the sea level rise observed so far. The major cause is thermal expansion: as the ocean has warmed, the water in it has expanded.

So, what of the future? The current annual rise (3 mm) would give a sea level increase of 26 centimetres by the year 2100. However, because temperatures are expected to rise, so too is the rate of sea level rise; consequently, most projections are higher than this, often in the vicinity of a metre. Due to various local factors, the rise is not expected to be even and, in general, is likely to be greater in the tropics (by 10–20%) and less in the polar regions.

A rise of one metre, with storm surges much higher, would, of course, cause a massive amount of damage and loss. Shore-based communities would face catastrophic problems. A 20-centimetre rise in sea level would render three-quarters of a million Nigerians homeless, and a 40-centimetre rise would put 11 per cent of Bangladesh's coastal land underwater, displacing seven to 10 million people. With a one-metre rise, 150 million people worldwide would be displaced: the Maldives would be uninhabitable; Tuvalu and other low-lying countries would be greatly at risk; major cities such as London, New Orleans and New York, which already need storm surge defences, would need more; highly productive river delta regions would start to be claimed by the sea; coastal infrastructure everywhere would become more susceptible to damage; and there would be large amounts of coastal erosion, causing some beaches to disappear and cliffs to crumble more frequently. Obviously, the economic and social cost would be huge.

But let's not stop there. Prior to the onset of the last ice age (120,000–130,000 years ago), the Earth experienced a warm period with temperatures for a time apparently higher than today. The sea level at this time reached a level four to six metres higher than it is now. A similar rise today would do unimaginable damage – many coastal cities would be decimated. Yet, as a species, we continue, each year, to add more CO_2 to the atmosphere than the previous year, and the ever-increasing CO_2 levels lock in ever-increasing temperature rises that lock in ever-increasing sea level rises. Will we stop before we lock in a six-metre sea level rise? The excuse that replacing fossil fuels with renewable energy sources in a major way cannot be done because it would cost a bit more is pitiful. It will not be looked on kindly by future generations, who will be disgusted.

It should perhaps also be noted here that if all the ice on the Antarctic land mass were to melt, the sea would rise by about 60 metres. The current Antarctic land-mass ice began to form 34 million years ago. The initiation of this land ice and its subsequent expansion was associated with declining levels of atmospheric CO_2.

Increasingly, governments fail to lead; instead, they check the polls and follow the pack. If the majority of the pack believes that increased greenhouse gas emissions will lead to global warming (and its many attendant problems), governments are more likely to act to reduce greenhouse gas emissions. One factor holding back the public's belief that it is time to act is the stance taken by at least one media mogul (and therefore by his media outlets) and the hosts of some talkback radio and television programs, who claim that global warming is not occurring or, if it is, will not be a problem. These people are wrong, and if they are taking this approach solely for short-term financial advantage or for some political reason, they should be widely condemned, for they are contributing to the stress, cost and likely loss of life that global warming will inflict on future generations. Many politicians also deny that greenhouse gas emissions are a problem; at least some of these are beholden, in one way or another, to the fossil fuel industry. They could be seen as traitors to humanity.

If those who currently argue that greenhouse gas emissions are not a problem are remembered in the future, it will likely be not in a hall of fame, but in a hall of infamy, and any statues erected to them will likely be designed to lie horizontally on the ground so people can spit on them, and wipe their feet on them, as they pass by. In the hall of infamy they will be in the company of the board members and executives of the major tobacco and asbestos-mining companies, Hitler, Stalin and Pol Pot.

18

Nightmare Scenario 2

Population Increase and Widespread Famine

A farmer planning to put some livestock into a paddock needs to take into account the carrying capacity of the paddock. Add too many livestock and they will eat the grass out completely, lose weight and die, and the topsoil, without its grass cover, will be eroded by wind and water. Add the right number of livestock, so that the grass eaten does not exceed the amount produced, and the livestock will likely be sleek and healthy, and the topsoil will remain intact – obviously the preferred outcome.

So, if we view the world as a paddock, and human beings as the livestock, what is the carrying capacity of the world? The answer depends on just how sleek we want our livestock to be. If we choose a level of sleekness that allows a family to eat well, live in a house or apartment with several fully-furnished rooms, including a large range of electrical goods, and own at least one car, we have problems because it has been calculated that 1.5 Earths would be needed to provide the resources necessary for all seven billion of us to live at this level. If we accept that the sleekness level just described is a reasonable one to aim for, we have to conclude that the world is already overstocked. The fact that already one billion of us do not have sufficient food would indicate that this is the case. Moreover, we need to remember that this is not a short-term stocking rate that we are considering, but one that needs to be sustainable for many generations into the future.

Given the constraints on food production outlined in Chapter 14, and the added difficulties that will come from the looming depletion of several large underground aquifers currently providing irrigation water, the exhaustion of phosphate reserves, rising sea levels and climate change, it is hard to be optimistic that we will be able to maintain even our current, low level of sleekness – especially since the world's population is expected to increase by two billion over the next 30 years. It is these facts that have led at least some experts in the field to suggest that famine, not just localised but widespread, is a real possibility within a generation or two.

Clearly, we are headed for difficulties in the near future, not just with food but also from the exhaustion of other resources and environmental degradation.

Clearly, the more people there are in the future, the worse these difficulties will be. Clearly, it would be a good thing if we could first stabilise the world's population and then start to reduce it. And yet, so many of our leaders in government and business, concerned only with short-term interests and personal gain, and either blind to or wilfully ignoring the consequences, continue to advocate population increases. More people means more sales (which business likes) – and a higher gross national product – to which politicians like to point.

The mindset of the politicians needs to be changed. One way to do this is to vote out of office politicians who advocate population increases, but this will only occur when a majority of the people are aware of the problems looming with the ever-increasing numbers of people. A good way to achieve this awareness is for well-known and respected individuals to speak out in favour of stabilising population levels.

Another possible way of changing the mindset of politicians is to point out to them that, increasingly, current and near-future problems associated with an ever-rising population might very well affect them negatively. These problems arise because, in an already crowded world, additional people add to the pressures and frustrations present in societies. For example, in undeveloped countries, pressure arises when one hectare of land has to feed more people than it did in the past. The higher prices that occur when there is a shortage of fuel or a particular food item, which is more likely to happen because of the higher population levels, often make people angry, especially if they are already on the breadline. This is usually not good for incumbent governments. In developed countries, governments frequently do not build the additional infrastructure that is required, or delay building it. Consequently, commuting times increase, parking is more difficult to find, queues and waiting times increase at medical centres and government services become harder to access. Frustrations build and people turn grumpy. Grumpy people vote out governments, even those that have otherwise done a good job. Really grumpy people, in both developed and undeveloped countries, can become angry. Riots and the burning of cars and buildings may follow, and this is not good for business or for governments. Politicians should be asking themselves whether population increases really are in their best interest – it could in fact be what will put them out of office at the next election.

So, let's dream again. We have a world that is governed by sensible, level-headed biologists, who recognise that the world is clearly overpopulated by humans. What would they do to rectify the problem?

One way would be to do nothing. Let the population go on expanding and then let nature take its course. Nature is very experienced at dealing with population explosions – it has handled millions of them. Large-scale death by starvation and/or disease and/or a build-up of predators are its favoured methods; but for humans it has, on occasion, introduced an additional control method: people killing each other as they fight for the limited resources remaining or vent their frustrations by attacking those of a different ethnic, tribal or religious group.

A second way to stabilise population levels is more humane. It is tried and proven and would almost certainly be adopted by our government of biologists. There are several elements to this approach.

1. Educate females – as more females enrol in secondary school, fertility falls.

2. Provide paid jobs for young women.

3. Increase the economic well-being of under-developed countries – "capitalism is the best contraceptive".

4. Make contraception cheap and readily available – as contraception rises, fertility falls.

5. Increase urbanisation, since urbanisation is usually accompanied by a decline in fertility. This, of course, is happening anyway – it is

not something that governments need to promote deliberately.

Fertility also falls as the age at which couples marry rises. However, because it is best for both mother and baby for a woman to have children while young (see Chapter 10), this may not be an approach followed by our government of biologists. Malaria and sexually transmitted diseases also reduce fertility levels, but no humane government would use disease as a tool to reduce fertility.

Clearly, implementing the steps outlined above will cost a great deal of money and take many years to accomplish. But the world really cannot afford not to try because the consequences of not stabilising and reducing population levels are horrendous.

19

Nightmare Scenario 3

Killer Oceans?

Fossil evidence indicates that there have been numerous mass-extinction events in the past 540 million years. In five of these events, over 50 per cent of animal species became extinct. With the exception of the event that killed off the dinosaurs 65 million years ago (caused, at least in part, by an asteroid impact) the cause(s) of these extinction events is not known with certainty. However, there is evidence that, at the time some of these extinctions occurred, the oceans were acidic and anoxic (oxygen depleted) and that species of shallow plankton that metabolised hydrogen sulphide (H_2S) were common.

An extinction theory based on these observations proposes that a large build-up of CO_2 and methane in the atmosphere (perhaps from massive volcanic eruptions) lead to acidic seas and produced a large global-warming effect. The increase in acidity, if high enough, would impair or prevent calcifying organisms from building their protective shells and skeletons (see Chapter 15); this could lead to some extinctions. In addition, the large global-warming effect would heat the upper layer of the oceans, thereby increasing the temperature difference between the upper and lower layers of the ocean, which would reduce or prevent mixing between the layers (a known effect). With no mixing, the lower layer would become anoxic because the oxygen dissolved in this layer would be used up by the animals and oxygen-requiring microbes living in this layer. The warmer surface layer would also contain less oxygen since less oxygen can dissolve in warm water than in cold.

As the lower levels of the oceans lost their oxygen, all animals living in this zone would die. If slugs of this anoxic water were brought to the surface, any surface animals that moved into this water would also die. This could account for the loss of many of the marine species observed in the extinction event. However, in the greatest of all the extinction events, which occurred 251 million years ago, not only did 90 per cent of marine species become extinct, but so did two-thirds of the land species. What killed off the land species? Here the clue comes from the finding of hydrogen sulphide-metabolising plankton at the extinction boundary.

In oxygen-depleted waters, bacteria that do not need oxygen can flourish. These bacteria use sulphate in place of oxygen and give off hydrogen sulphide. If whole oceans, or large sections of them, became anoxic, large amounts of hydrogen sulphide could be produced by the sulphate-using bacteria, which could directly affect land as well as ocean life. Hydrogen sulphide is a highly poisonous gas affecting several different systems in the body, but particularly the nervous system. Above 50 ppm, damage can start to occur to humans, and above 320 ppm, death becomes a possibility. Depending on the concentration, hydrogen sulphide can also damage and kill oxygen-producing plants and, being an ozone-destroying gas, can deplete the ozone layer, thereby allowing more ultra-violet light to reach the Earth's surface. Thus, hydrogen sulphide has the ability to impose a range of stresses on land-based life. If a build-up of hydrogen sulphide in the atmosphere did kill off two-thirds of land species 251 million years ago, it could do so again.

Blooms of hydrogen-sulphide-producing bacteria are not just a theoretical possibility. They have been observed in modern times in the Dead Sea and in the Atlantic Ocean off the coast of Namibia. In the Namibian case, the bloom stretched about 150 kilometres along the coast and occurred when a large amount of oxygen-poor water reached the coast. Thus, the global warming we are generating by continuing to pour CO_2 and other greenhouse gases into the atmosphere might do more than just change the climate and raise the sea level: it could end up, via blooms of hydrogen-sulphide-producing bacteria in the oceans, directly harming humans and the life systems on Earth that support us. But, ho-hum, this is only a possibility and it won't affect our generation, so let's not bother ourselves by changing any of our current practices.

Hydrogen sulphide, which has the stench of rotten eggs, has been released from the sea off the coast of the Namib Desert since at least the nineteenth century. Here, great blooms of phytoplankton occur due to an upwelling of nutrient-rich water. Zooplankton, which would normally control such blooms by feeding on them, fail to do so here because strong winds push water and the slower-breeding zooplankton offshore before they have time to consume the bloom. When the huge numbers of unconsumed phytoplankton die, they form a deep sludge on the sea floor that becomes anoxic as oxygen-consuming bacteria begin to decompose the sludge. When this occurs, the sulphate-using bacteria reign supreme, generating large quantities of hydrogen sulphide. As a result, people living on the nearby coast have to live with the stench of rotten eggs.

20

Nightmare Scenario 4

Death by Microbe

Antibiotics kill bacteria. In medicine, being able to kill bacteria is very useful. Diseases caused by bacteria can be cured and bacterial infections that might otherwise occur after surgery, childbirth and cancer treatments can be prevented. Without antibiotics, simple things can kill. In 1921, the author's grandfather, at the age of 35, developed a boil on his nose. The infection spread to his bloodstream causing his death – he left a wife and three young children. Boils begin when a bacterium, commonly *Staphylococcus aureus*, infects a hair follicle. Boils can be cured by antibiotics. If antibiotics had been available in 1921, my grandfather would not have died.

So, what is the problem? Well, the problem is that health authorities are increasingly warning that the era of antibiotics could be about to end. Words such as "apocalypse" are being used. Why? Because the disease and infection-causing bacteria are increasingly becoming resistant to the antibiotics currently available. In some areas, antibiotic-resistant bacteria are increasing to such an extent that they are starting to grow out of control. Until recently, bacteria that were resistant to all the commonly used antibiotics could be controlled by a class of antibiotics called carbapenems – the antibiotics of last resort. However, bacteria that are also resistant to these antibiotics are now appearing. These really are superbugs. In developed countries, stringent isolation of people carrying such bugs may limit their spread. But in developing countries, this does not occur – it is open slather for the bugs. Clearly, the potential exists for the human species to be hit by a bacterial apocalypse. Clearly, the world urgently needs new antibiotics – ones to which bacteria have not been exposed previously. Given the urgency of this need, is the world working flat out to find and develop new antibiotics? Well, no. Since 1990, a majority of the major pharmaceutical companies have stopped working on antibiotics. Why? It's all economics: regulations require that the final trials to establish a drug's effectiveness be large (involving thousands of people) and such trials are expensive. Antibodies do not make the companies much money because, typically, people take a set course of tablets and that's it. In addition, new, effective antibiotics tend to be used sparingly, typically as a last resort, to try to limit the chances of resistant bacterial strains arising.

The boards of the pharmaceutical companies should perhaps reconsider, take a wider view, and ponder the consequences of what would happen if there were a worldwide explosion of fully antibiotic-resistant disease and infection-causing bacteria. Instead of seven billion people to whom to sell their highly profitable drugs, there might be far fewer. That definitely would not be good for their bottom line. Taking this view, developing new antibiotics could be seen as insurance for the rest of the company's more profitable operations.

Although there are apparently no new antibiotics ready to be released, some hope remains for the longer-term future. Researchers in universities have discovered potential new antibiotic candidates. All that is required is funding to run the necessary trials. If private enterprise will not fund them, surely governments should step in and provide the necessary funds. It would be money well spent. Some governments are starting to engage with the problem, but 10 years late. Once again, governments have failed to listen to what scientists have been telling them. Once again, it is only at the eleventh hour that they decide to address the problem. We really do need more scientists, especially biologists, in governments.

As frequently pointed out, the widespread and routine use of antibiotics in the chicken and livestock industries has greatly facilitated the rise of antibiotic-resistant bacteria. These antibiotics are commonly used not to control disease, but to speed up growth for greater profits. Profits for a few while putting the whole of humanity at risk – absolute stupidity. But weak-willed governments, looking only at the short-term advantage while ignoring long-term disadvantage, are good at doing stupid things. They should be careful, however, because there may come a time when their actions are no longer viewed as short-sighted and self-serving, but as criminally negligent.

21

A PLEA

Humans are an intelligent species. Through our knowledge of physics and chemistry, we have an understanding of the physical world around us. Through our studies of the living things on this planet and how they interact with each other and with environmental factors, we also have a good knowledge of the biological world around us. These two knowledge sources put our species in a unique position: we can start to determine elements of the future. We can say that if we follow one course of action, X is likely to happen, whereas if we follow another course of action, Y is likely to happen. If X is judged to be the preferred outcome for our future, we can choose the path that will likely lead to that outcome. We are a clever species – in theory!

In practice, however, we often behave as the dumbest of species. We are on a path that our intelligence tells us will almost certainly lead to grief. We know what we need to do to avoid or diminish this grief, but we do next to nothing. No government has, as yet, recognised the seriousness of our situation and put their country on a war footing, in which the war to be fought is one against environmental and social calamity. Ignorance, failure to heed the word of scientists, belief systems, vested interests and short-term political and economic goals are all reasons governments do little to divert us from the path to catastrophe. Some things can be done at the grassroots level; but only governments, acting in concert around the world, can have a meaningful influence on the huge environmental problems that are, and will, affect us. We wait, and wait, for governments to act. Unfortunately, given the nature of our present governments, we are likely to wait in vain. Pity us and our descendants.

Is there a government somewhere, anywhere, that will lead? Please.

Sources

This essay covers a wide range of topics. Although the author has consulted some original scientific papers, he has mostly relied on secondary sources such as articles and news items in science magazines such as *New Scientist, Scientific American, Australasian Science, Cosmos* and *American Science* and in newspapers. For the ecosystem management chapters, Julian Cribb's book *The Coming Famine: The Global Food Crisis and What We Can Do to Avoid It*, Callum Roberts's book *Ocean of Life*, the CSIRO report *Climate Change: Science and Solutions for Australia*, the Australian Academy of Science report *The Science of Climate Change* and Wikipedia were also used as valuable sources of information.

www.ingramcontent.com/pod-product-compliance
Lightning Source LLC
Chambersburg PA
CBHW031213270326
41931CB00006B/552

* 9 7 8 1 9 2 2 2 0 4 6 7 7 *